Skies of My Dreams

Skies of My Dreams

Poems by

Kathy Abrahams

Acknowledgements

Some of these poems first appeared in the following publications:
Australian Writers' Journal, *Breath of the Eucalypt*, *Centoria*,
The Dawn, *FreeXpression*, *Gentle Reader* (UK), *Lucidity* (USA),
Micropress Oz, *Readers' World*, *Vermont Ink* (USA).

One poem was read at the Voice Coffee Literary Café.

Skies of My Dreams
ISBN 978 1 74027 125 7
Copyright © text Kathy Abrahams 2002

First published 2002
Reprinted 2017

GINNINDERRA PRESS
PO Box 3461 Port Adelaide 5015
www.ginninderrapress.com.au

Contents

The Writer	7
Writers' Inspiration	8
Word Desert	9
Imagination Muscle	10
Nocturnal Wings	11
Poetry	12
Birth of a Poem	13
Still Birth	14
Essence of Femininity	15
Liberated Woman	16
Boa Constrictor	17
Desire's Demon	18
Arctic Promises	19
Lovers' Spat	20
Wounded Pride	21
Jungle Predators	22
Agitation	23
Shawl of Indifference	24
Fleeting Cloud	25
Faded Flower of Youth	26
Old Age	27
Pendulum of Fate	28
A Queen	29
Tragi-queen	30
Wounded Butterfly	31
Leaves of Days	32
Soul Sanctuary	33
Mirror Portrait	34
Serendipity	35
Empty Shell	36

Microcosm	37
Leafy Tranquillity	38
Summer-sun Ogre	39
Winds of Change	40
Conscience's Ghost	41
Compassion's Flower	42
Reconciliation	43

The Writer

Brows furrowed by concentration,
Pen poised,
Fired by creativity's demon.

Thought breeze stirs,
Perspiration beads glisten under
Rays of creative sun.

Words ooze from pores,
Spill onto pages.
Literary storm.

Writers' Inspiration

Vivid imagination,
Writers' gold-lined treasure chest
Of sparkling literary gems
Waiting to be unearthed.
The key of inspiration lifts the lid,
Seizes a lustrous gem of an idea,
Crafts it,
Brings a polished brilliance forth,
Bedazzling captive readers
With jewels of their art,
Enlightening them, delighting them.

Word Desert

Dry inkwell of imagination
Parched desert of paper awaiting
Droplets of words to
Bloom into literary flower.

Imagination Muscle

Imagination muscle chilled,
Words frozen,
Pages naked,
Cold, yearning
For warmth from
Drape of words.

Nocturnal Wings

Nocturnal gold gossamer wings of fantasy
Fly me high above the skies,
Land my feet on a fragrant velvety carpet of rose petals.
The sweet delicate wine of a cacophony of bird song
Pours into the cup of my ears as I tiptoe through the
Petalled paths of the wonderland of my imagination.

Poetry

The beautiful sounds of poetry's violin
Caress my spellbound ear.
So touching, so tender,
A skilful procurer of tears.
Treasured crafted pieces,
Thought tapestries of the poet,
The haunting resonance of their
Melodies lingers on forever.

Birth of a Poem

Words   images   rustle leaves of creativity
        In a sudden breeze of imagination
A whirlwind of words spins from mind yarn
        Poem seeds fall on page

Still Birth

Gravid with child, motionless she sits,
Drooping head upon her protuberance consoling the decayed
    seed within.
Black-fingered death grips its neck,
Seals its fate within a hearse.

Essence of Femininity

I am female,
Gold-spun silk cloth of the essence of femininity
Drapes upon my nurturing shoulders.
Tender butterflies, wings dipped in the oil of love,
Compassion, guidance and comfort,
Fly from fragrant bushes of my heart,
Brushing cheeks with womanhood's reassuring touch,
Strengthening, uplifting, healing.
I am female, the essence of femininity,
Steel backbone of man.

Liberated Woman

She drags the weight of the kitchen sink off her mind
Pots and pans shackles of steel forging domestic bind
A knife of pain stabs her breast
Suckling infant depletes milk supply
Diaper demands press an urgent button at the other end
Arriving nanny scoops child away
Showering   the stale scent of morning
Swirls down the plug hole as she
Plans to alight upon another landscape of her day
Donning pinstriped business-suited armoury
She prepares to do battle in a jungle of wolves
Cache of feminine wiles polished and poised
With sharp fangs
She seals deals with winking eyes
Pitting her wits in a den of male counterparts
Firing ammunition of ideas into the decision-forming
Front line

Boa Constrictor

Boa constrictor of my desire for you
    Scales dipped into a silver paint of fantasy
Coiled itself around my heart spring
    Constricting its pulse
Suns of make believe glowed on the skies of my dreams
    With each daydream the coils squeezed
    Tighter   tighter
    My breaths became
    Weaker   weaker
My limp body captive to your power
Boa constrictor of my desire for you
    Squeezed breaths of sanity from me

Desire's Demon

Desire's demon ignited a
Fire of folly
Within my breast.
Flames of scorching fire
Leapt higher   higher.
Sails of reason's abandonment billowed on a
Boat of self-gratification,
Resting its anchor in
Cooled waters of ardour.

Arctic Promises

Promises of love from
Your Arctic frozen heart
Chill me

Your wind voice pierces
My eardrums

Iced words trap me in a cave of
Sub-zero temperatures
Where stalagmites
Of anguish knife me

Your ill-wind ceases
I begin to thaw
Slowly rising from a
Melting tomb of heartbreak ice

My feet walk upon
Exit steps ascending from
This abyss of despair
Withdrawal from your presence
My Eskimo suit of defence

Lovers' Spat

Barrage of ammunition fires
From your machine-gun mouth.
Like a bombed battleship,
I flounder beneath waves of words.
Retreating from gunfire,
I set sail on a life raft and head
For the shores of a
Sun-tonic island of solitude.

Wounded Pride

Verbal darts pierce the
Silken fabric of the soul.
Fragmented, it falls down
A blackened hole.
Pride's wounded serpent
Raises its head,
Flickers its venomous tongue.

Jungle Predators

You encroach upon my territory
Eyes flashing   claws ready to strike.
Adrenalin rushes   I hiss
My fur bristles   I bare my teeth.
We stand in dense scrub
Of our personality clash,
Crouching   poised.
Wondering who will
Be the first to
Go for the jugular.

Agitation

Emotions spinning in
Tumble drier on mid-life cycle.
Spin, spin, spinning
All around.
Up, up, and down.
Washed out
Wrung out.
Clicked on.
Safety switch.

Shawl of Indifference

She presses her nose
Against the rain-lashed window
Eyes glazed with pain
Leaves quiver and fall

She wraps the shawl of
His indifference around her shoulders

Winter's season begins within

Fleeting Cloud

Momentum of time
Sways rocking chair
Back and forth

Tired eyes gaze
At the sunset horizons
Of his years

Memories of dark ghosts loom
Followed by smiling maidens
Waving greetings as in
Days gone by

Tears   bittersweet drop into a
Cup of sighs.
'Life,' he whispers, 'a fleeting cloud.'

Faded Flower of Youth

Fallen petals from youth's faded flower
Freeze between the wispy whisper of lament's sigh.
She bows her head in mournful pose,
In sweet remembrance of former days when
Youth's honeyed kisses gave her cheeks a rosy glow,
Lit her countenance so.
Closing the book of reflection,
She opens her eyes and turns her head,
Her forward steps ascending mid-life's spiral stairway.

Old Age

Links of sluggishness
Enchain her mortal frame,
Her weary bones slaves
To the master of time.
Seated   limp arms dangle beside
A tree trunk of a body,
Legs rooted to the floor.
Wisps of lament blow through
Her nostrils as she languidly speaks,
'Technically, I'm not a young woman any more.'

Pendulum of Fate

Right gongs for prosperity,
Left for adversity.
Barometric pressure of
Life's season of fortune.
Tick-tock, life's clock,
Ebb and flow.
Fate's pendulum swings.

A Queen

No jewelled crown adorns
        her head
Her fingers curl around a
Broomstick of a sceptre
No luxurious gown clothes
        her in
Royal ostentation

Well-worn faded memories drape
        from her shoulders
A modest home is her Palace Royal
With loving discipline she rules
        her subjects
Her family loyal

She walks upon a red carpet of their
        reverence with pride
They bow before her placing her on
        her Royal household throne

Tragi-queen

Rueful bars of pensiveness cage her thoughts.
Black dress of mind skirts over the mirror of her life.
Banshee wails echo amongst hills and valleys of tragedy.
Reflection spirals land her tiny feet at its base,
Cracked silver shards appear,
Babyhood days wrapped up in a coarse rug of neglect.
Toes twirl over broken slivers to reach the mirror's centre.
Fragments of parental rejection shine.
Pain's raging river engulfed her soul.
Leaping up higher, her doleful eyes spot bigger slivers,
Death's hand snatched a loving spouse and infant child.
Scenes of betrayal by two other partners loom,
A chattel used then heartlessly tossed aside.
'Fate, why did you treat me cruelly?' she cries.
Penniless and forlorn in her twilight years, and in
Failing health, she watches as the remaining glass
Splinters into slivers.
Sunken eyes reveal melancholia's rouge on her pallid face.
A tarnished silver crown adorns her greying hair
On it she reads: 'Tragi-queen.'

Wounded Butterfly

Wounded butterfly with a
Broken wing,
She crawled into my life.
Searched my face with
An intent gaze.
Faded into
Obscurity's night.

Leaves of Days

Spent leaves of days from the trees of our lives
Spiral softly downwards each nightfall,
Falling gently to the ground.
Fanned by the steady cool breeze of time.
Falling leaves of days,
Some tinged with the gold glitter of happiness, some with silver,
Others glisten with teardrops of sadness,
Heartache and anguish etched onto their cracked dry surfaces.
Falling leaves of days,
Constantly falling through the years until the last chapter
In the book of our lives has reached the final page.
Down below, the Master Weaver of time sighs
As he stands back and admires
Each and every richly woven autumnal-toned
Leaf carpet beneath the now spindly trees.

Soul Sanctuary

Within the inner haven of my soul,
A gold enveloping mist of peace cocoons its heart.
Perfume from a heavenly potpourri sweetens the air.
Angels transport my heart to infinite heights of ecstasy.
Piercing thorns of worry fall.

Mirror Portrait

Crystal page of soul
Reflects in mirror.
Portrait of solemnity.
Glass-kissed whisper.

Serendipity

I walk upon the
Branches of the tree
Of my life,
Reflect upon its gnarled trunk,
The hollows   twists
Dryness of bark.
A breeze of fate stirs,
Blanketing the ponderous silence.
Gold leaf flutters down   kisses my cheek.
I bend   scoop it up,
Its silken touch caresses my palm.
My pulse quickens.

Empty Shell

An empty shell,
She stands on
The edge of a
Mountain of sorrow,
Eyes focused downwards:
'Should I jump into
The sea   into oblivion
Shatter this empty shell?'
She pauses   reflects:
'Will dawn's light pierce
The blackness
With a knife of hope?'
Taunting whisper
Glues her feet to the rock.

Microcosm

I, a microscopic speck
Of the universe,
Flow steadily along
In its stream.
Not rippling the surface,
Unimpeding the flow.
Swimming in the direction
Of the current of my dreams.

Leafy Tranquillity

Despair's darkness spins a
Web around my troubled mind.
Psyche's fingers grope along its
Cavern walls seeking
Peace's enlightened gem.
Weary soul lays me upon
Nature's verdant balm.
Tongues of comfort and
Reassurance speak from
Rustling leaves.
Gentle breezes of answers
Whisper upon my brow.

Summer-sun Ogre

The summer-sun ogre ravages the tender beauty
Of the fair earth child.
Scorching streaming rays of fire drain the
Rosy-red colour from her parched cheeks,
Wrinkled sunburnt leather dons
The landscape of her once blooming face.
The verdant velvet gift of a frock fashioned by
Mother Nature smoulders in
Tatters of crisp burning black
Draping heavily from her smoking frame.
Lost in yearning gold dreams of desire,
Her hot dry lips drink in
Life-giving water from a brimming
Silver goblet of autumn rains.

Winds of Change

Icy cold winds of truth
Blow across the city
Of the pipe dreams
In my mind.
A cutting razor-sharp blade
Of stark reality slashes the
Sky-high towers of my schemes
With such precision.
Amidst the rubble,
Hot sulphuric tears flow.
There are pangs of indecision.

Conscience's Ghost

The ghost of conscience haunts the dimly lit
Corridors of temptation castle.
Chilling shrieks of warning flash
Stop lights of red
Within the walls of the psyche.
Eyes of night see this
Nocturnal spectre floating airily
Gowned in a robe of purity's white,
Zealously seeking to protect
Character's moral treasure of gold,
Stopping the heels of souls
From slipping into
Sin's darkened pit.

Compassion's Flower

Droplets of pain
Spilling from the
Fountain of
The soul imbues a
Deep shade of colour
Into compassion's flower,
Imparting a fragrance of
Healing to scorched hearts.

Reconciliation

Waters of reconciliation
Submerge hardened hearts
In the appeasing flow
Of its current.
Seeds of bitterness,
Anger and hatred wash away
In the ebb and flow
Of its tide.
Storm clouds
Of dissension dissipate.
Harmony's sun shines
Within its gold sphere.

www.ingramcontent.com/pod-product-compliance
Lightning Source LLC
Chambersburg PA
CBHW062206100526
44589CB00014B/1986